ENCYCLOPEDIA
of
ME

MY LIFE FROM

A *to* Z

AMY KROUSE ROSENTHAL

potter style
NEW YORK

A    B    C

G    H    I

POTTER STYLE

Copyright © 2014 by Amy Krouse Rosenthal. All rights reserved. Published in the United States by Potter Style, an imprint of the Crown Publishing Group, a division of Random House LLC, a Penguin Random House Company, New York.

www.potterstyle.com

Potter Style and colophon are registered trademarks of Random House LLC.
ISBN 978-0-8041-8612-4

Cover and interior design
by Danielle Deschenes
Cover and interior illustrations
by Jeffrey Middleton

Printed in China
10 9 8 7 6 5 4 3 2 1
First Edition

M    N

R    S

W    X

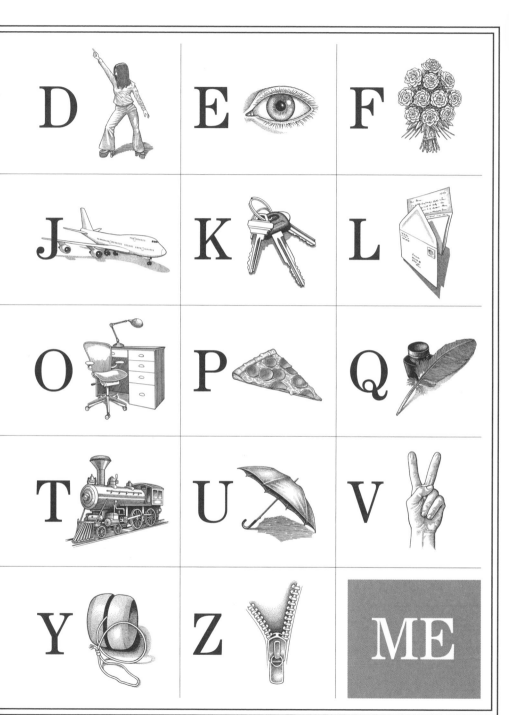

ABOUT THIS JOURNAL

Almost immediately upon publication of my "alphabetized memoir" *Encyclopedia of an Ordinary Life*, I began hearing from readers who were inspired to use the tidy A–Z structure to create their own personal encyclopedias. Some versions were short and sweet. Some were elaborate and filled with images as well as writing. Some were collaborations between family members, friends, or classmates. But they all followed the same simple premise introduced in my book: thoughts and memories organized alphabetically.

Over the years I've heard from individual journalers, scrapbooking groups, book clubs, and families. I've heard from high school English teachers who assigned A–Z encyclopedic writings. I've heard from college writing professors who assigned it as a final paper. I've even heard from elementary school teachers, including one in Washington, D.C., who sent me a copy of his class's charming *Encyclopedia of an Ordinary 3rd Grade*.

I have to admit, this *"Hey, I want to do that!"* response had not occurred to me when I wrote the book. But, of course, it made perfect sense once I saw it set in motion.

All this backstory is to say: I don't know how it took me eight years to realize that the encyclopedia format could make for a pretty nifty guided journal.

I do so love the full-circle nature of this: a book that inspires its readers to create something, which in turn inspires its author to create something. And here we are.

A couple of quick notes on the design of this journal. You'll find a mix of lined pages, list-y pages, and wide-open blank pages to be used in whatever way strikes your fancy— drawings, stick-figure sketches, doodling, affixing a photograph or memento, word art, or, of course, continued free writing. As for the prompts at the top of each page, if you come across any that don't speak to you, promise me you'll scratch them out and write in your own.

In terms of pacing, some may be inclined to fill out the journal in a few power sessions; others may prefer to spread it out over time. Alphabetical fun fact: with twenty-six letters, savoring one letter section a week would have your journal complete in exactly half a year.

Here's to all the *Encyclopedia of an Ordinary Life* readers who shared their subsequent (and fabulous) encyclopedias with me.

And here's to your own encyclopedic journal experience . . . may it be filled with everything from Affection to Zeal.

Amy Krouse Rosenthal

Acknowledgments

A ffirmations worth meditating on, a few positive

- _____
- _____
- _____
- _____
- _____
- _____
- _____
- _____
- _____
- _____

- _____
- _____
- _____
- _____
- _____
- _____
- _____
- _____
- _____
- _____

Again, did it but don't need to ever do it

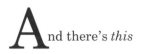

And there's *this*

Angry, man oh man was I ever

See also: Emotions

A nnoying, things I find incredibly

- _____
- _____
- _____
- _____
- _____
- _____
- _____
- _____
- _____
- _____

- _____
- _____
- _____
- _____
- _____
- _____
- _____
- _____
- _____
- _____

Anticipating, what I am

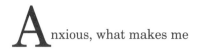

Anxious, what makes me

- _____
- _____
- _____
- _____
- _____
- _____
- _____
- _____
- _____
- _____

- _____
- _____
- _____
- _____
- _____
- _____
- _____
- _____
- _____
- _____

A

pology, I owe this person an

See also: Forgive

Applause, why I could use a little

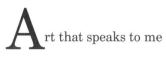

Art that speaks to me

Awwwwkward

Bacon, a few words about

B ad movie, I can't help watching it even though I know it's a

Table No. 1

BANDS I SO LOVE

Bedroom, memories of my childhood

See also: Childhood, a bit about my

Best day, all-time

Best friends, past and present

- _____
- _____
- _____
- _____
- _____
- _____
- _____
- _____
- _____
- _____

Bio, in 100 words or less here is my

B

ittersweet, this memory (sigh) really feels

_____

_____

_____

_____

_____

_____

_____

_____

_____

_____

_____

_____

_____

_____

Books, my shelf of favorite

B orn, about the day I was

Brag

areer

Table No. 2

CEREALS OF MY YOUTH

Cereal	Memory

Certainty, this I can say with

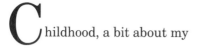
Childhood, a bit about my

Table No. 3

CITIES	
Love These	Would Love to Visit These

Clothing, cherished items of

Coincidences

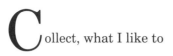ollect, what I like to

College

Colors I am drawn to

- _____
- _____
- _____
- _____
- _____
- _____
- _____
- _____
- _____
- _____

Concerts, a few of my favorite

- _____
- _____
- _____
- _____
- _____
- _____
- _____
- _____
- _____
- _____

Cook, what I first learned to

Could, I would if I

C

ry, things that tend to make me

- _____

- _____

- _____

- _____

- _____

- _____

- _____

- _____

- _____

- _____

See also: Tears

Dad

Dating

See also: Heartbreak; Romance

D
eal breaker, I'm flexible and forgiving but this is a

Death, my feelings about

Decisions, one of the hardest

Deserved it

D ied, I often think of these people who have

_____

_____

_____

_____

_____

_____

_____

_____

_____

_____

_____

_____

_____

_____

Dinner

Dream house

Dreams

E

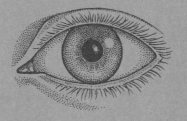

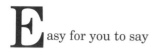

Easy for you to say

Embarrassing

motions

Table No. 4

EMOTIONS	
Use These	Don't Use These

Epic win

rase, a moment I wish I could

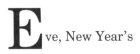ve, New Year's

See also: Resolutions

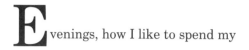
Evenings, how I like to spend my

Everyday joys

- _____
- _____
- _____
- _____
- _____
- _____
- _____
- _____
- _____
- _____

- _____
- _____
- _____
- _____
- _____
- _____
- _____
- _____
- _____
- _____

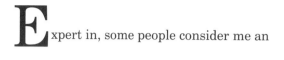xpert in, some people consider me an

Table No.5

EXTRACURRICULAR ACTIVITIES

Past	Present

Eyes, it's been said about my

F

F

ailure, my relationship with

See also: Epic win; Humble; Victory

Family

F avorites, a list of

- _____
- _____
- _____
- _____
- _____
- _____
- _____
- _____
- _____
- _____

- _____
- _____
- _____
- _____
- _____
- _____
- _____
- _____
- _____
- _____

Fears

Firsts

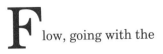

Flow, going with the

F lowers you should definitely get me

Food, glorious

See also: Dinner; Lunch, what's for; Meal, what a memorable; Recipe; Yuck and yum

orgive

Future, ten years into the

G enetic, what can I tell you, it's

Gifts, treasured

Goals

-
-
-
-
-
-
-
-
-
-

- _____

- _____

- _____

- _____

- _____

- _____

- _____

- _____

- _____

- _____

G od

Gold, this is pure

Gorgeous

See also: Everyday joys

Grandparents

Grateful

GROCERY LIST

Always Get	Always Forget

Gullible

H

Habits

H andwriting styles, just for fun let's try a few

- _____

- _____

- _____

- _____

- _____

- _____

- _____

- _____

- _____

- _____

Hanging out, who I am with

_____

_____

_____

_____

_____

_____

_____

_____

_____

_____

_____

_____

_____

eartbreak

ell, my idea of

Heroes

High school

Hindsight

Home

Hopes

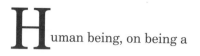

Human being, on being a

Humble

Ignorance

I

ll, what makes me feel better when I feel

Independence

Instant gratification

- _____
- _____
- _____
- _____
- _____
- _____
- _____
- _____
- _____
- _____

Table No. 7

INSTRUMENTS	
Play	Wish I Played

I nvention?, wouldn't this be the best

I sh

Island, what I want on a desert

I tching to do, things I'm

Jobs

- _____
- _____
- _____
- _____
- _____
- _____
- _____
- _____
- _____
- _____

okes

See also: Ha!

J ourney, how I feel so far about my life's

J oy, jump for

Just barely

Justification

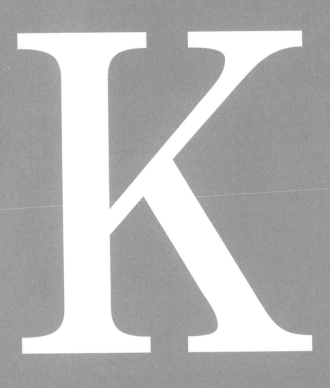

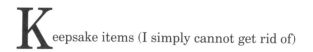
Keepsake items (I simply cannot get rid of)

- _____
- _____
- _____
- _____
- _____
- _____
- _____
- _____
- _____
- _____

Key dates

- _____
- _____
- _____
- _____
- _____
- _____
- _____
- _____
- _____
- _____

- _____
- _____
- _____
- _____
- _____
- _____
- _____
- _____
- _____
- _____

Kindness

_____

_____

_____

_____

_____

_____

_____

_____

_____

_____

_____

_____

_____

_____

See also: Grateful

Kitchens, memories associated with

See also: Home; Neighbors

Kryptonite

Languages I can speak/je peux parler/peudo hablar

- _____
- _____
- _____
- _____
- _____
- _____
- _____
- _____
- _____
- _____

Leisure

Lies I told

List, and now . . . a totally random

- _____
- _____
- _____
- _____
- _____
- _____
- _____
- _____
- _____
- _____

- _____
- _____
- _____
- _____
- _____
- _____
- _____
- _____
- _____
- _____

Lonely, thoughts on being alone vs. being

Lost

Love

Lunch, what's for

Lyrics?, aren't these great

M

Magic, something about this just felt like

Marriage

M_{ate}

Meal, what a memorable

Midlife, what better time than the exact middle of the journal to share my thoughts about where I am/hope to be at

M
ind, random things that for some reason often come into my

- _____

- _____

- _____

- _____

- _____

- _____

- _____

- _____

- _____

- _____

- _____
- _____
- _____
- _____
- _____
- _____
- _____
- _____
- _____
- _____

Miracle, if this happened it would feel like a

Mistakes, I've really learned from these

M_{om}

See also: Dad; Siblings

More, what the world needs is

Morning routine

Mouth, took the words right out of my

Movies

See also: Bad movie, I can't help watching it even though I know it's a

N

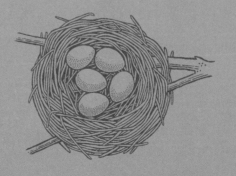

Name, here's how I feel about my

_____

_____

_____

_____

_____

_____

_____

_____

_____

_____

_____

_____

Nature, where I go to immerse myself in

Necessities vs. wants

Neglect, what I will never

Neighbors

New

Table No. 8

NICKNAMES	
Childhood	Adulthood

Nostalgia

N

othing, what I'm doing when I'm doing

Observations

Obsessions as of late

- _____
- _____
- _____
- _____
- _____
- _____
- _____
- _____
- _____
- _____

- _____
- _____
- _____
- _____
- _____
- _____
- _____
- _____
- _____
- _____

O
bvious now, it didn't seem so then but it sure seems

Ode

Office, just another day at the

See also: Career; Jobs

O
ff, these things turn me

- _____
- _____
- _____
- _____
- _____
- _____
- _____
- _____
- _____
- _____

Old, what makes me feel

Once upon a time

O pen-minded

O

pinion, I often/rarely give my honest

Organized, I am so/I am so not

Over it

Parties

Pets

Philosophy

Pizza

P_{lay}

P oems

See also: Ode

Politics, let's talk

Prepared, sure wish I had been better

Table No. 9

PRESIDENTS	
Favorite	Not So Favorite

Pro/con

- _____
- _____
- _____
- _____
- _____
- _____
- _____
- _____
- _____
- _____

- _____
- _____
- _____
- _____
- _____
- _____
- _____
- _____
- _____
- _____

Procrastinating

Questions

Quiet, places I go for some peace and

_____

_____

_____

_____

_____

_____

_____

_____

_____

_____

_____

_____

_____

_____

_____

_____

_____

See also: Zen, when I feel most

Quirks

- _____
- _____
- _____
- _____
- _____
- _____
- _____
- _____
- _____
- _____

- _____
- _____
- _____
- _____
- _____
- _____
- _____
- _____
- _____
- _____

uits, called it

Quizzical

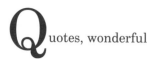

Quotes, wonderful

- _____
- _____
- _____
- _____
- _____
- _____
- _____
- _____
- _____
- _____

R

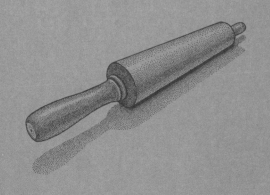

Recipe

Regrets

Remember

R esolutions

- _____
- _____
- _____
- _____
- _____
- _____
- _____
- _____
- _____
- _____

Restaurants

Review, super-quick year in

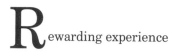

Rewarding experience

Roadblocks

Romance

Scars

School memories and mates

Self-portrait

Siblings

Sigh

Significance, things of strange

- _____

- _____

- _____

- _____

- _____

- _____

- _____

- _____

- _____

- _____

Smells that are strongly associated with certain memories

Social media, the "me" in

Sorry but I'm not sorry

Spirit animal, my

Sports

Struggles

See also: Ups (and downs)

Stupid, times I felt

Superstitions

- _____
- _____
- _____
- _____
- _____
- _____
- _____
- _____
- _____
- _____

Talents, hidden

Tantrums, temper

Teachers

Tears

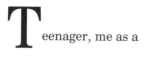Teenager, me as a

See also: High school

Tomorrow, what I'll probably be doing

_____

_____

_____

_____

_____

_____

_____

_____

_____

_____

_____

_____

Travels

See also: Wanderlust

Treat, what feels to me like a

_____

_____

_____

_____

_____

_____

_____

_____

_____

_____

_____

_____

_____

Trust, people I can truly

U

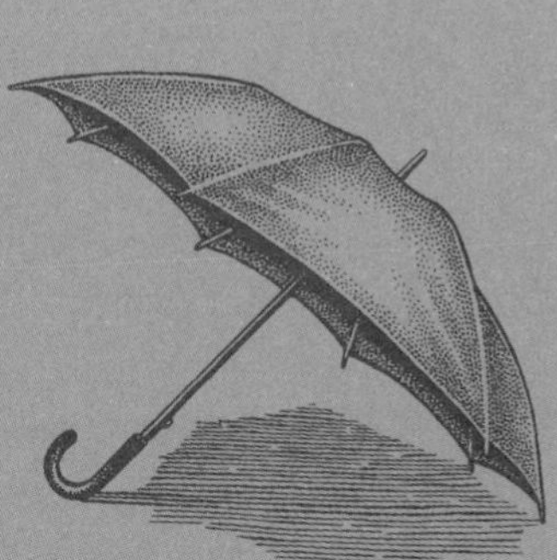

Ugh

U nanimous, it's

Underrated

Understood, I wish I

U ndo, I wish I could

_____

_____

_____

_____

_____

_____

_____

_____

_____

_____

_____

_____

_____

_____

See also: Mistakes, I've really learned from these;
  Prepared, sure wish I had been better; Regrets

Unknown fact

Ups (and downs)

U s

Vacation

Values

V enn diagram, my life expressed as a

ery

Veto

Vicariously, living

Victory

iews

V ocabulary, show-offy highlights of my

- _____
- _____
- _____
- _____
- _____
- _____
- _____
- _____
- _____
- _____

Wanderlust

Wardrobe

See also: Clothing, cherished items of

Weird things about me

- _____
- _____
- _____
- _____
- _____
- _____
- _____
- _____
- _____
- _____

- _____

- _____

- _____

- _____

- _____

- _____

- _____

- _____

- _____

- _____

Window

Wisdom

ishes

See also: Hopes; Yearn

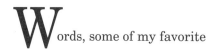

Words, some of my favorite

- _____
- _____
- _____
- _____
- _____
- _____
- _____
- _____
- _____
- _____

Worldview

Worst

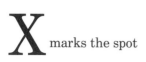
X marks the spot

X^O (sending hugs and kisses to my friends and family)

See also: Love

X-rays

- _____
- _____
- _____
- _____
- _____
- _____
- _____
- _____
- _____
- _____

X

X or XY (perks of being a girl or boy)

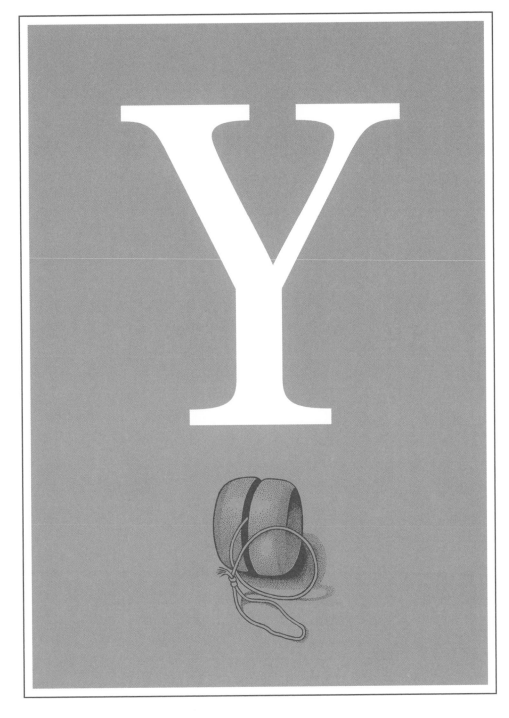

Yawn, thought it'd be fab but it was a big

Yay!

Yearn

Yet, one day I hope for this but it just hasn't happened

You

Youth

Yuck and yum

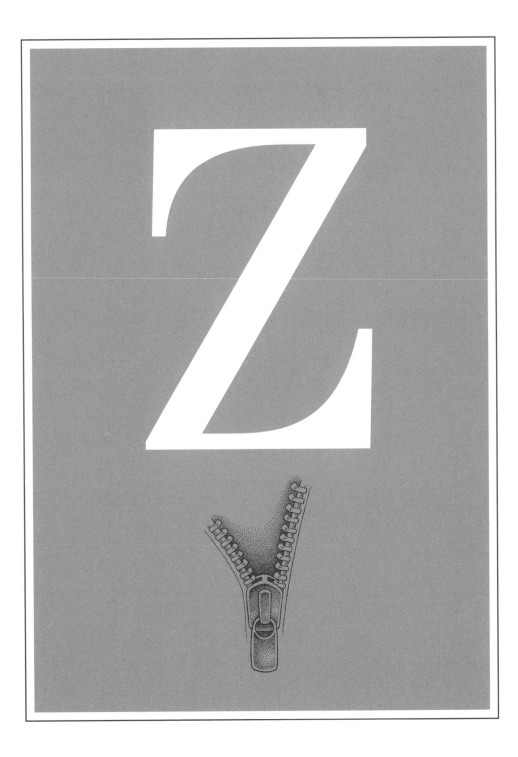

Zen, when I feel most

Zigzaggy, wrapping up in a manner that's stream of consciousness and

Zip codes, where I've lived according to

Z zz (good night)